# MAKING CALLIGRAPHY WORK FOR YOU

Tom Barnard
Christopher Jarman

## An Osmiroid Book of Ideas

## About the Authors

# Tom Barnard A.R.C.A.

Tom Barnard is a graduate of the Royal College of Art and a craft member of the Society of Scribes and Illuminators. Tom has 26 years experience as a consultant in penmanship to education and the trade. Tom is currently employed by Osmiroid, touring the country demonstrating calligraphy and undertaking television and radio broadcasts.

# Christopher Jarman M.Ed.

Christopher Jarman has been teaching handwriting for more than 25 years as a Primary School Teacher, Headmaster, Lecturer and Education Adviser and now as Head of In-Service Training at the Roehampton Institute of Higher Education in London. Christopher has been Handwriting Adviser to Osmiroid for the past 20 years.

### Acknowledgement

Grateful thanks to all Calligraphers and Publishers for their permission to use works, which are individually acknowledged.

### © E S Perry Ltd., 1985

# Contents

# Making Calligraphy work for you

Calligraphy is the art of beautiful writing. The written word has been with us for thousands of years in many forms, and as by definition a record is to be kept, writing became the art of presentation too. In this way pictures and words have always been closely related, often combining to become part of one another to present a message. In fact, the origins of our present day alphabet were the hieroglyphic symbols of ancient civilisations. The alphabet of one civilisation was adapted by the next and evidence of these historical differences are still to be seen in the marvellous brush inspired letters of the Far East and the Arabic alphabet of the Middle Eastern countries, which was in use and reached perfection long before civilisation came to the West; it eventually underwent further changes and filtered into the West through the spread of the Roman Empire. Presented with these variations we can observe how imagination and the eye for the aesthetic, through the centuries, provided a wealth of ideas and beautiful examples of lettering.

After the invention of printing, the art of Calligraphy diminished and remained dormant until the end of the last century when it was revived by William Morris and carried on into this century by Edward Johnston, who along with other enthusiasts founded the Society of Scribes and Illuminators which has continued to promote an awareness of the craft during the 20th century. The Society for Italic Handwriting has also been active in promoting good handwriting in recent years. Today the craft is a thriving contemporary art in its own right.

Today when computer typesetting and video displays communicate the bulk of information, the hand written effect of Calligraphy is increasingly becoming more appreciated and people of all ages are rediscovering the pleasure of using the straight edged writing instrument, which for centuries played such a key role in developing the Western form of legibility and examples of Calligraphy of great beauty which we can still admire today.

This book has been published to show how varied and practical the skill of Calligraphy can be and hopefully to provoke the interested person to 'have a go'. All that is required is a suitable pen, paper and patience; there are many good instruction books available and with the recent proliferation in the number of Calligraphy courses being offered, the beginner does not have to look far for help.

The enjoyment of the execution of good Calligraphy must be within the parameters defined by a disciplined approach, but at the same time the scope for individuality and creativity is enormous. There is always a new idea, a new approach or a greater degree of skill to strive for and this is part of the fascination of the craft. Calligraphy is a pursuit for the individualist and more often than not the satisfaction gained is purely personal. This should be an encouragement to the beginner who need not feel under pressure to achieve any standards but his own.

# Certificates and Diplomas

Perhaps the best known use of the Calligrapher's art, whether serious or lighthearted, a certificate or diploma will be a keepsake for a lifetime.

## Royal Academy of Arts

### Royal Academy Schools
### Postgraduate Diploma

Awarded to

Roger Charles Conlon

by the President and Council

at the conclusion of a three year course

in the School of

Painting

A. Specimen
PRESIDENT

Henry Bloggs
VISITOR

C. Signature
KEEPER

A.N. Other
SECRETARY

17 June 1978

(Original 44 cm x 31.5 cm, Coat of Arms in gold )          *John Woodcock*

# THE ROYAL RUGBY CLUB

## OF THE COUNTY OF WARWICKSHIRE

This certificate is given to record the very excellent
standard of sportmanship rendered on the field by

and is presented by the Club Manager and Club Members on
the first day of May Nineteen Hundred and Eighty Five

SPORTSMAN CLUB · IN · GREAT BRITAIN

CLUB MANAGER

CLUB SECRETARY

*Tom Barnard*  7

*In appreciation of the kindness and help rendered by*

_____

*The*

**KINGFISHER CLUB**
*records it's sincere thanks*

_____

_____

*Tom Barnard*

8

# Menus

An attractively presented menu will enhance a meal, borders and Calligraphic patterns can add interest to the presentation.

*Tom Barnard*

# Menu for St.Valentine's

Candle-lit dinner served Friday February 11,
Saturday February 12 & Monday February 14
from 7pm: also Sunday February 13, noon - 2.30pm.

## FIRST COURSE

Eve's Salad  or
Cream of mushroom soup  or
Eggs Valentine

## MAIN COURSE

Chicken with Broccoli
in creamy cheese sauce
or
Partridge breast braised
with bacon and mushrooms
or
Hungarian-style Pork with paprika and
caraway

## PUDDINGS

Strawberry Mousse
or
Coupe Venus (with our own-made ice cream)
or
Valentine Gâteau  (served on 14 February only)
and Cheeseboard:
heart-shaped Neuchatel or spiced Dorset cheese

Coffee and our own sweetmeats

£5.75  including service and V.A.T.

*Gerald Sweetman*

# Place Names

Seating plans and place names have a practical purpose, why not make them attractive too?

Tom Barnard

*Tom Barnard*

# Invitations

We all receive invitations from time to time to a wide variety of functions, here you see both the formal and the less formal.

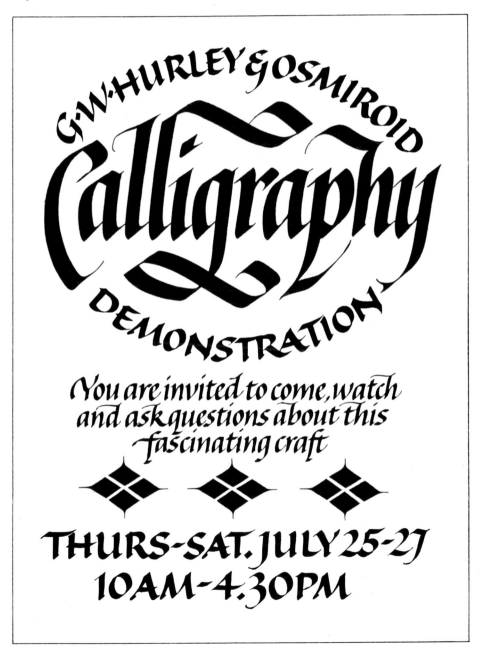

*Tom Barnard*

Harrods

Calligraphy

WEEK

Osmiroid Pens welcomes

you to this Demonstration

NAME _____

March 19th. to 26th. 1985

*Tom Barnard*

The Society of Scribes & Illuminators request the honour of your attendance at an Illustrated Lecture by Ieuan Rees·M·De·RCA· on Wednesday·11·March·1981·at·7·15·p·m· on

# The·Versatility·of·Lettering·&·Calligraphy

In Lecture Theatre A·Room 213·Huxley Building·Imperial College of Science & Technology·London SW7· Entrance in Queen's Gate·The Chair will be taken by Rev·Stanley Knight

R·S·V·P
The Hon Secretary SSI
Ann·Vue·Camomile Lane
5·The Barbican Road
London SW15·6NL

*Ieuan Rees*

*Ron & Alice*

invite you to their
**ENGAGEMENT PARTY**
on Friday May 10th.
at the
Roebuck Hotel at 8p.m.

*Evening Dress*

R S V P

*Tom Barnard*

# Christmas Cards

Many people make their own Christmas cards. Sometimes they are hand-drawn or made with cut paper designs or lino prints. The problem with pictorial cards is that one quickly runs out of ideas – candles, robins, holly and so on, are quickly exhausted. With a calligraphic card not only can you use an infinite variety of messages, poems, sayings, verses from hymns and quotations, you can make up your own words. In addition to this variety you can often form the word block into a logo or Christmas shape too. Simply fold a piece of A4 paper into four and make your design in one quarter. Send it to the local printer to print on any colour paper in any colour ink, and don't forget to order matching envelopes.

*Christopher Jarman*

*John Smith*

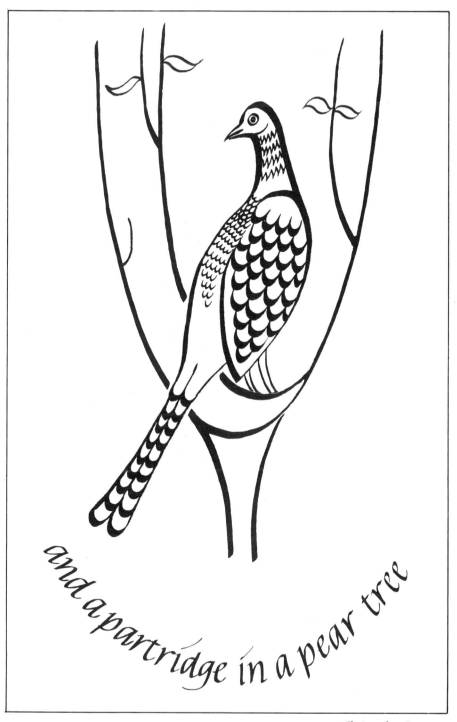

*and a partridge in a pear tree*

*Christopher Jarman*

*John Smith*

*Elizabeth and Frank Cryer*

# Posters and Notices

Most posters and notices are produced in small quantities maybe for a local event. In these cases it is advisable to use a waterproof ink if the posters are to be used outdoors. If you prefer to use non-waterproof ink you can cover a notice in plastic film such as is used for bookjackets, or you may try painting a layer of P.V.A. adhesive over the poster. Another way to help waterproof calligraphy (or watercolour painting) is to rub the work all over with the side of a wax candle which will coat it with a waterproof layer (this is particularly good for dealing with addresses or envelopes which you wish to smudge-proof).

For posters and notices which are to be printed or reproduced by photo-copying, it is possible to use white gouache or typists correction fluid to tidy up the design before printing.

*Tom Barnard*

The Book Arts Tradition & Craft

DONALD JACKSON
KATHRYN & HOWARD CLARKE
PETER WATERS · SHEILA WATERS
DEBORAH EVETTS · ISMAR DAVID
RODERICK STINEHOUR
PHILIP GRUSHKIN

NEW JERSEY · FALL 1977

*Alice   From Modern Scribes and Lettering Artists*
*Published by Trefoil Books Ltd*

AND DEMONSTRATIONS OF

AN EXHIBITION

calligraphy

BY ANN HECHLE

URBAN STUDIES CENTRE
ABBEY CHAMBERS BATH

EXHIBITION OPEN:- DECEMBER 7 - JANUARY 3 | MON - FRI · 8·30 - 5·0 P.M.
DEMONSTRATIONS:- DECEMBER 12·13·14·21·22 | 10·30 - 12·30 : 2·00 - 4·00

# Chichester Festival July & August '85

One of the Cathedral cities of England whose historical roots are Roman, but it is also an unspoilt Georgian Town

# PROGRAMME of EVENTS AND TICKETS FROM INFORMATION OFFICE

*Tom Barnard*

Tom Barnard

# Wine Labels

Commercial wine labels have always been used to create an image of respectability, authenticity and dependability. This means that usually in German wines the old Fraktur or Black Letter styles predominate giving an historical style to the label. In France the most respected older names will have a discreet drawing of the Chateau and perhaps an engraved Copperplate style of writing. Occasionally a little heraldry or a crest or achievement of arms is included in the label design to give a personal authority to the wine.

For amateur wine makers, all these subtleties can also be employed, especially for the fun of it. The local stream or ditch can be taken as the river by whose side the grapes were either trodden or bought in a kit! A heavy red elderberry could have thick gothic lettering to indicate its seriousness, and a light but effective parsnip wine could be labelled in a formal italic. Wine labels also give marvellous scope to the invention of mock crests or drawings of English suburban "chateaux".

*Christopher Jarman*

·V·VERIWOOD CHATEAU·V·VINTAGE CIDER·V·
1984 BREW

1·9·8·5
PRODUCE OF GERMANY
Rheinpfalz
Liebfraumilch
Qualitätswein b.A
FREDERICK WEIHNACHTSMANN GmbH BERNKASTEL WEHLEN

*Tom Barnard*

27

# Book Plates

You can always write your own name in the front of books that you own, if you become famous your signature may increase the value. Calligraphic book plates with the sign Ex Libris or from the collection of …….. can be individually named bookplates and make very attractive and welcome gifts; making them to order can be quite profitable. What is more, unlike Christmas cards, bookplates are welcome all the year round.

*Christopher Jarman*

*Tom Barnard*

*Irene Alexander*
*From Modern Scribes and Lettering Artists*
*Published by Trefoil Books Ltd*

# Calligraphic Drawings

Drawing and Calligraphy are closely allied, indeed the history of the alphabet started by drawing the object represented and which, for the sake of convenience gradually developed into symbols. Drawing was very much a part of the early hand produced book and this gave an added richness to the written page. This is still true of contemporary Calligraphy and what could be a visually dull page can be enlivened by adding appropriate drawings with a fine straight edged nib, particularly if a second colour is used.

One source of inspiration is to look at some of the pages of the early manuscripts to see how drawings were used, or to be more practical obtain some black and white drawings or photographs of say, trees, people or animals and see if you can render them in simple outline with a fine nib, removing all the necessary detail. Another idea is to reverse the historic process and design a picture using letters only, with patience this can give some spectacular results.

*Tom Barnard*

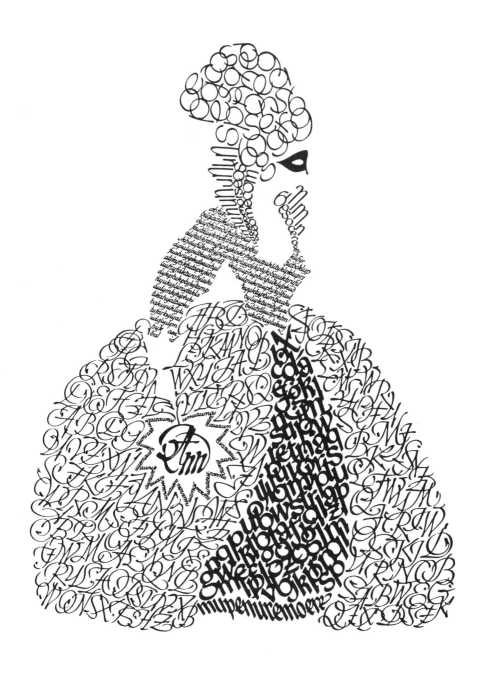

*"Ann" Villu Toots*
*From Modern Scribes and Lettering Artists*
*Published by Trefoil Books Ltd*

Tom Barnard

31

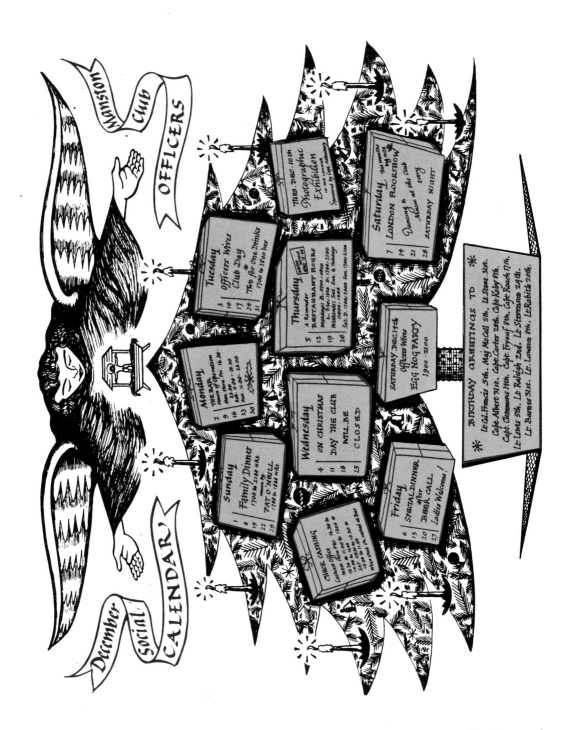

*Tom Barnard*

# Logos

The Alphabet has often encouraged artists to be adventurous, today the logo made up of initials or a whole word has often taken the place of the heraldic device. It is said that the word 'elemental' meaning "basic" or "central" was made by the Romans from the central three letters of the alphabet.

A logo in calligraphy may be a simple sketch or series of lines exploiting the ribbon-like thick and thin nature of the edged pen.

*Tom Barnard      Christopher Jarman      Ieuan Rees*

# Decorative Calligraphy

The alphabet can be beautiful in its own right but the desire to decorate has always been strongly evident throughout human history. The Western letter forms are only one of a number of alphabets used by various nations around the world and even if the language is not understood, the different visual textures on the page can be very pleasing to the eye. This is certainly true of the Far Eastern brush written characters and the flowing pen forms of the Islamic cultures. Studying these sources as well as the medieval European manuscripts will suggest fresh ways of using Calligraphy in a decorative manner.

*Tom Barnard*

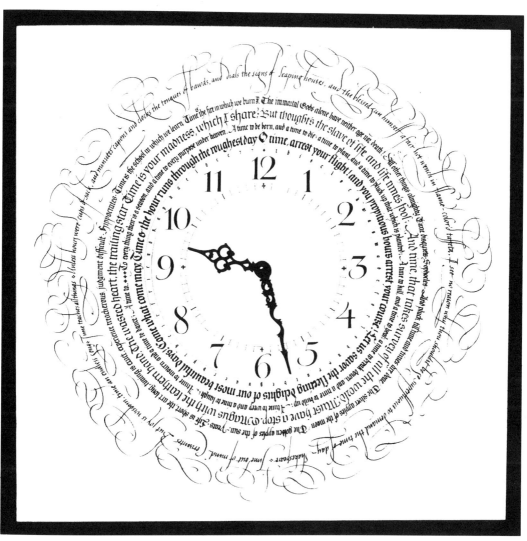

*Raphael Boguslav*
*From Modern Scribes and Lettering Artists*
*Published by Trefoil Books Ltd*

*Ghani Alani*
*Calligraphy composition THULUS JALIL*
*and RAIHAN, from a mystical chant*
*Soufi to the glory of the Divine*
*Uniquity.*

*Tseng K'e-tuan*
*From Contemporary Chinese Painting*
*and Calligraphy*

# Business Cards and Stationery

Today we have come to accept as normal, printed calling cards, business cards and letterheadings using various forms of mechanical type face. With modern high quality instant printing facilities or even high quality photocopyiong, more individualised styles of card can be designed. Calligraphy when well done can make your own cards or compliment slips unique. Remember that calligraphy produced for reproduction will look crisper if reduced by about 25% from your original artwork. Also, it is possible to paste together the best of your trial efforts and tidy them up by using typists correction fluid. Unless a piece of calligraphy is intended to be seen in its original form it is quite pointless to try and write it out neatly all in one go, do not be afraid to try-out, cut up, paste and touch up.
A calligraphic design can be used to produce a house style.

SAM SOMERVILLE — Calligraphy & Gilding
abcdefghijklmnopqrstuvwxyz · AbcdefghijklmnopQrstuvwxyz
14 CAMBORNE ROAD · MORDEN · SURREY · SM4 4JJ · ENGLAND
TELEPHONE: 01-540 1796

abc
defghijklmnopqrstuvw
xyz
DAVID WILLIAMS
119 Langley Way · West Wickham
Kent BR4 0DL
01 777 7272
CALLIGRAPHY
FOR OCCASIONS THAT NEED
NICE WRITING

Calligraphic
Workshop:
CERTIFICATES · AWARDS
CHANGE OF ADDRESS CARDS
INSCRIPTIONS &
INVITATIONS
All kinds of writing
25 · EASTVILLE · CLAREMONT RD
BATH · AVON
TEL: BATH 314052

LINDSAY CASTELL
C A L L I G R A P H E R
44 CROCKERTON RD · LONDON SW17 7HG
PHONE 01-767-6615

**CHARLES BLOSSUM** — Member of the Horticultural Society — Est. since Nineteen Hundred & Five

**Flower and Gardening Centre**
THE COPSE WELWYN HERTFORDSHIRE
Telephone 612773          Director C. Blossum

July. 25th. 1985

Dear Mr. Greenhand,

Thank you for your recent letter of July. 27th.

The items you request will be processed within the next

two days, except for the bags of peat which we are regretfully

‾ing a fresh supply towards the end

‾ deliver to your address as soon

‾nclosing a copy of our

‾ur future patronage.

‾s faithfully,

*Charles Blossum*

**CHARLES BLOSSUM** — Member of the Horticultural Society — Est. since Nineteen Hundred & Five

**Flower and Gardening Centre**
THE COPSE WELWYN HERTFORDSHIRE
Telephone 612773          Director C. Blossum

**Flower and Gardening Centre**
THE COPSE WELWYN HERTFORDSHIRE
Telephone 612773          Director C. Blossum

**CHARLES BLOSSUM** — Member of the Horticultural Society — Est. since Nineteen Hundred & Five

**Flower and Gardening Centre**
THE COPSE WELWYN HERTFORDSHIRE
Telephone 612773          Director C. Blossum

*Tom Barnard*

# Envelopes

Everyone likes to receive a personally addressed letter, imagination and a little thought will yield well accepted results.

# Doodles and Fun with Calligraphy

There is no end to the design possibilities inherent in playing about with words and pens. The interest lies in trying to achieve an effect that could not be done any other way, that is without an edged pen. The use of contrasting sizes of nibs makes for dramatic effects of scale.

*Christopher Jarman*

# Recipes

Recipes will be kept and used sometimes for years, so why not make them interesting to read too? Some pieces like the examples here, when framed, would make an attractive addition to any kitchen wall.

sage · marjoram · saffron · dill · thyme

chicory · borage · purslane · samphire · rue

sorrel

camomile · tansy · bergamot · savory · basil · mint

dill · rosemary · hyssop · fennel · lovage

## THYME
### Thymus Durius

Time has an agreable aromatic smell and a warm pungent taste & is grown as a pot herb & used where Rosemary or Sage are usually employed. The odour of Time hath the qualities of Camphor.

There be two sorts of Garden Time among the old writers, the latter Herbarists have found more. Thymus Durius, or Common Garden Time is so well known that it needeth no description.

Time boiled in water and honie, and drunken is good against the cough & shortness of breath

*Rosemary Sassoon*

43

# Quotations

Many people have a favourite quotation or passage, Calligraphy can bring it to life. It is interesting to give thought to the many design possibilities offered by different layouts.

RISE UP MY LOVE
MY FAIR ONE
and come away;
For lo, the winter is past,
the rain is over and gone;
The flowers appear on the
earth; the time of the
singing of birds is come
and the voice of the turtle
is heard in our land:
The fig tree putteth forth her
green figs, and the vines
with the tender grape
give a good smell
Arise, my love, my fair one,
and come away.

From Canticle of Canticles. Chapter 2. o'Sullivan scripsit, '79

*Alex O'Sullivan*

Caricature is the
the tribute that mediocrity
pays to genius

I often quote myself
it adds spice to a
conversation

Brevity is the soul of wit

Everyone is ignorant
only in different subjects

Argument is
the worst sort
of conversation

IF
BOTTICELLI
WERE
ALIVE TODAY
HE
WOULD BE
WORKING
FOR
VOGUE

Live hard die young
and have a beautiful
corpse

Every dogma must
have it's day

A rich man's joke is
always funny

To me, old age
is always fifteen years
older than I am

Short neck - good mind

Genius is born not payed

Originality is
nothing but
judicious imitation

Ambition
is the last refuge of
failure

Any fool can
criticise and many of them do

QUOTES POT POURRI

*Tom Barnard*

45

# Music Calligraphy

Music Calligraphy has both practical and artistic sides, the examples shown here show some ideas as to how the Calligrapher can add variety.

**SVPERIVS. PSEAV. VI. CL. MA.**

N Evueille pas ô Sire, Me reprédre en ton

ire, Moy qui t'ay irrite: Në ta fureur terrible

Me punir de l'horrible Tourmēt, quay merité

**TENOR**

N Evueille pas ô Sire, Me reprédre en ton

ire, Moy qui t'ay irrite: Në ta fureur terrible

Me punir de l'horrible Tourmet, quay merite

*Tom Barnard*
*From Clément Marot 1496–1544*

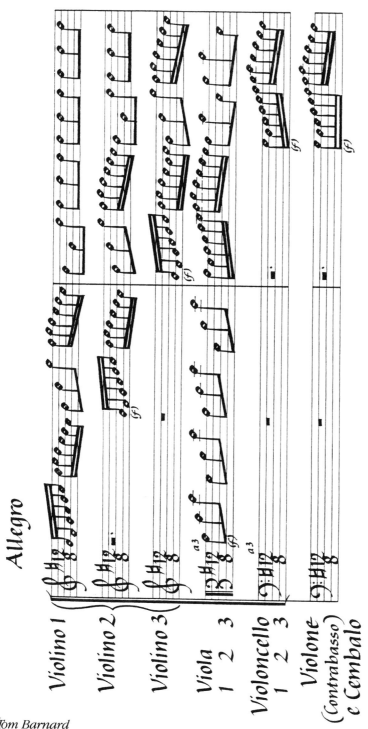

Allegro

Violino 1
Violino 2
Violino 3
Viola 1 2 3
Violoncello 1 2 3
Violone (Contrabasso) e Cembalo

*Tom Barnard*
*From J. S. Bach 1685–1750*

47

# Title Pages

As the introduction to a book, the title page can reflect the mood of what is to follow, with the variety of alphabet styles and patterns available to the Calligrapher this can easily be achieved.

*Tom Barnard*

# Family Trees

If you are fortunate enough to have this information about your family, a Calligraphic record would preserve it for your descendants.

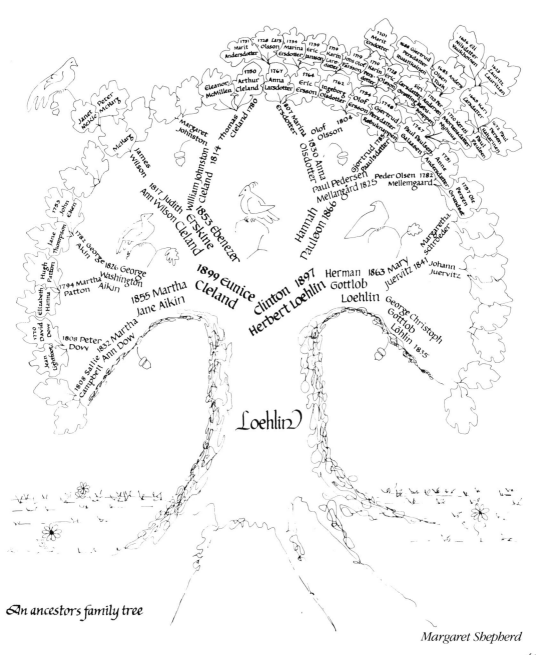

An ancestors family tree

*Margaret Shepherd*

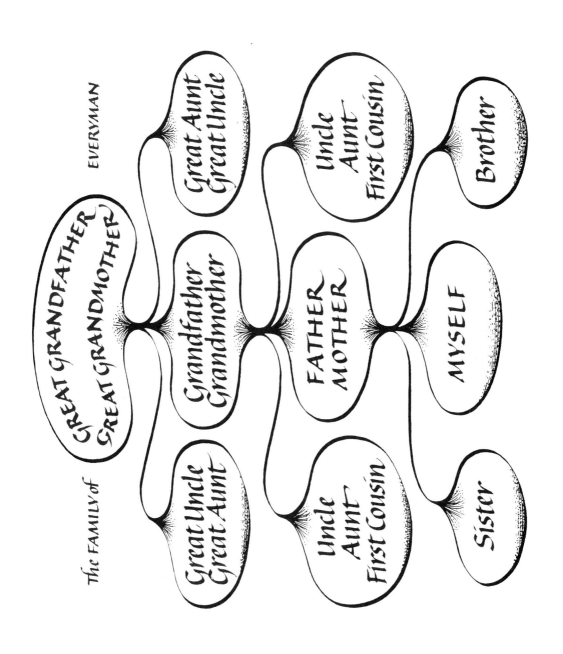

EVERYMAN

The FAMILY of

Tom Barnard

# Maps

Maps and charts have historically provided much scope for the inventive, the geographic information often supplemented by lavish titles and illustration. The Dutch cartographer Gerard Mercator used the italic hand for his maps, a style that has often been imitated. The same pen or quill used to draw the map may be used to write both capitals and italics, this tends to give aesthetic coherence to the drawn map or chart. These engraved examples may provide inspiration.

*Susanna Fisher, Upham*

Redoute

St Pierre

A
B

les Cordeliers

B

15

le Port                    Fanal
15              le Mole
                    Petit Fanal sur
12        12      la Jettee neuve
15        30
10
Mont
l'Arsenal
ou
Tressane

Couvent

VILLE NEUVE

PLAN DE BARCELONE
Capitale de Catalogne.
A   Palais du Vice Roy
B   La Maison de Ville.
C   L'Hopital
Echelle de Quatre Cent Toises
100    200    300    400

MONT JOUI

*Susanna Fisher, Upham*

# Heraldry

Heraldry is the complex art of designing and carrying out armorial bearings or achievements of arms. Even today wherever you look in a town street you will see the shields and crests of banks and other big businesses which carry on the herald's tradition. Your county council and your local public house may well show arms of some sort or another. These badges or identity marks spring historically from the need for one armoured knight to distinguish another, in particular friend from foe in the heat of medieval battle.

*Ronald Pidgley*

# Sand Blasting

This technique can be used for applying Calligraphy to glass. The design is photographed and the positive or negative is transferred on to a silk screen from which an inked paper stencil is produced. This is then stuck on to the glass and when dry is put into a cabinet and blasted with sand, under pressure. The ink acts as a barrier and only the exposed parts of the design are reproduced onto the glass.

*Tom Barnard*

# Letter Cutting

Although letter cutting is really the province of the professional, the beginner should not be deterred. The examples shown here are all chiselled in slate (not an expensive material), the lettering being given prominence with white painting or by being gilded with gold leaf.

SWAKELEYS

On 2nd May 1984
Her Majesty The Queen
opened the first
International Garden Festival
held in Great Britain

To
commemorate
the opening of Elmwood Court
this plaque was unveiled by
The Ambassador
of the United States of America
the Honourable Charles H. Price II
on Thursday 16th May

1985

*David Baker*

# Tips for Folding

### How to select suitable paper for a manuscript book

Take a sheet of paper you would like to use for your book & cut it exactly the same size. Fold it carefully into two pages and crease it with a bone folder along the spine. If the paper curves over & stays down by its own weight it is suitable.

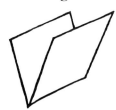

If the paper stands up it is too thick.

### Planning a single section book

A section normally consists of four book sheets, eight leaves or sixteen pages.

p1-2, 15-16 End papers
p3 Title page
p5 Beginning of Book
p12-13 End of Book
p14 Colophon

All downward measurements taken from the Top cut edge, all horizontal measurements taken from the spine outwards.

a. Top or Head of book, a cut edge.
b. Deckle may be left on Foredge and Foot of Book.

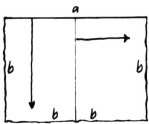

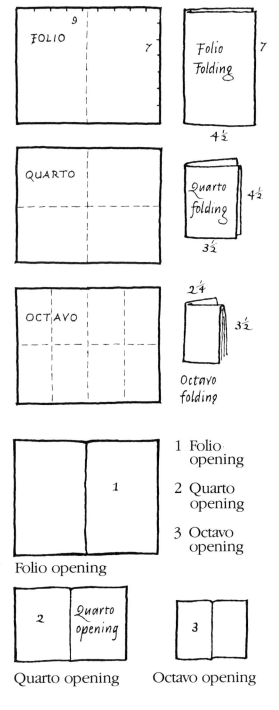

1 Folio opening

2 Quarto opening

3 Octavo opening

Folio opening

Quarto opening          Octavo opening

# Stitching

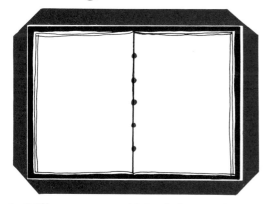

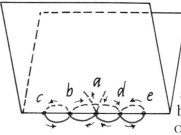

This diagram represents the folded sheets of a single section book and the outer cover.

The method of stitching with a strong needle & thread a single section book.

1 Stiff outer cover ⅛ inch larger than book

2 Coloured paper 3 inches wider than outer cover all round.

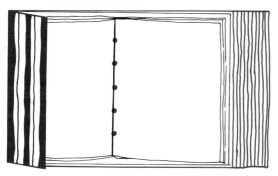

3 Bound as book above but with a decorative outer jacket overlapping the left and right foredge by 3 or 4 inches.

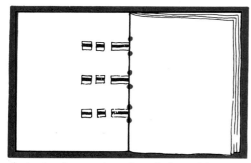

4 A single section book laced by tapes or paper strips to the cover of the book.

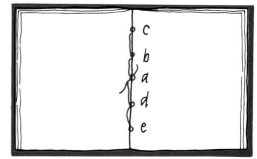

Pass the threaded needle from the centre of the book at a through to the back cover, leaving a length of thread inside; insert needle into the book at b, out again to the cover at c, back once more at b, and across to d & through to the back at d, into the centre at c, out once more at d & in at a. Check that the tension of the stitches is correct, tie the two ends with a knot over the long thread & cut off the thread about half an inch above knot.

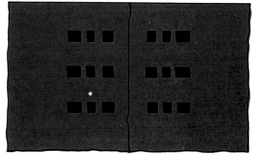

The back of a single section book laced by tapes or paper strips.

# Margins

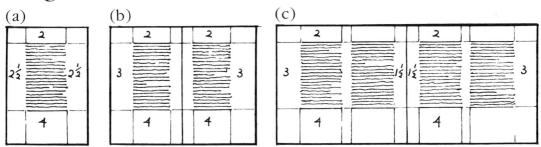

(a)             (b)                       (c)

A single sheet    A Double-page Spread    Oblong book: with double columns
or broadsheet     Upright book

Proportions of margins for (a) Broadside; (b) Upright M.S. Book:
(c) Oblong M.S. Book.

| | | 2 HEAD MARGIN | | | 2 HEAD MARGIN | |
|---|---|---|---|---|---|---|
| 3 | FOREDGE MARGIN | 1 2 3 4 5 6 7 8 9 10 11 12 13 — Length of Text Column — | INNER MARGIN | INNER MARGIN | ←— Width of Text Column —→ | FOREDGE MARGIN 3 |
| | | FOOT MARGIN 4 | 1½ | 1½ | FOOT MARGIN 4 | |

VERSO                RECTO

| | 1 2 3 4 5 6 7 8 9 10 11 12 13 | | | | |
|---|---|---|---|---|---|
| | HEAD MARGIN | T E X T  C O L U M N | | FOOT MARGIN | |
| ←SIDE MARGIN→ | ←WIDTH OF TEXT COLUMN→ | INNER MARGIN | INNER MARGIN | ←WIDTH OF TEXT COLUMN→ | ←SIDE MARGIN→ |

pp 56–58 *Dorothy Mahoney*
*From the Craft of Calligraphy*

# In Conclusion

The art of Calligraphy was 'lost' for 500 years until it was revived in the last century, and although its original function of producing books has been taken over by new printing technology, it is a craft that fascinates an increasing number of people. It is significant that the present interest in Calligraphy is not coming down from the top, but is a theme which has captured the imagination of the public at large. Nostalgic images of learning how to write at school, and the uncreative influence of electronic systems of communication provide some of the answers to this phenomenon. As in many areas of human activity it is the knowledgeable amateur who is the life blood of the movement.

This book has not set out to illustrate unattainable standards but to show that Calligraphy is a skill within the reach of most people and to show you how to put the skills you have learnt to satisfying and practical uses.

# Range of Nibs

OSMIROID produce the world's largest range of fountain pen nibs for fine writing, calligraphy, drawing and music writing.

## Regular Right Hand

Rola Extra fine

Rola broad soft.

italic medium

Rola fine soft

italic extra fine

italic broad

Rola medium soft.

italic fine

## Specialist Right Hand

Rola medium hard.

Long life tipped nib

Copperplate

SH4

SH5

SH6

B2

B3

B4

B5

B6

B8

B10

## Regular Left Hand

*Rola medium soft*

*italic medium*

*italic broad oblique*

*italic fine oblique*

*italic medium oblique*

## Specialist Left Hand

**B2** *oblique*

**B3** *oblique*

**B4** *oblique*

# INDIA INK

*Sketch*

*Rola medium soft.*

**B2**

*Sketch* BOLD

*Rola broad soft.*

**B4**

*Music*

*italic medium*

**B6**

Many of the nibs illustrated are obtainable in a range of pen sets manufactured by Osmiroid for calligraphy, italic writing, drawing and sketching.

# Arabic Available in Sets

عريض ٢
**Broad 2**

عريض ٣
**Broad 3**

عريض ٤
**Broad 4**

عريض ٥
**Broad 5**

عريض ٦
**Broad 6**

رفيعة جدًا ولينة
**Very Fine Flexible**

رفيعة اكسترا
**Extra Fine**

رفيعة
**Fine**

متوسطة
**Medium**

عريضة
**Broad**

# Calligraphy societies

## Calligraphy societies in USA and Canada

Calligraphers Guild
P.O. Box 304, Ashland, OR 97520

Calligraphy Guild of Pittsburgh
P.O. Box 8167, Pittsburgh, PA 15217

Capital Calligraphers
332 Atwater S, Monmouth, OR 97361

Chicago Calligraphy Collective
P.O. Box 11333, Chicago, ILL 60611

Colleagues of Calligraphy
P.O. Box 4024, St. Paul, MINN 55104

Colorado Calligraphers Guild
Cherry Creek Station, Box 6413, COLO 80206

Escribiente
P.O. Box 26718, Albuquerque, NM 87125

The Fairbank Society
4578 Hughes Road, RR3 Victoria, B.C.,
Canada V8X 3X1

Friends of Calligraphy
P.O. Box 5194, San Francisco, CA 94101

Friends of the Alphabet
P.O. Box 11764, Atlanta, Georgia 30355

Goose Quill Guild
Oregon State University, Fairbanks Hall,
Corvallis, OR 97331

Guild of Bookworkers
663 Fifth Avenue, New York City, NY 10022

Handwriters Guild of Toronto
60 Logandale Road, Willowdale, Ontario,
Canada M2N 4H4

Houston Calligraphy Guild
c/o 1024 Willow Oaks, Pasadena, TX 77506

Indiana Calligraphers Association
2501 Pamela Drive, New Albany, IND 47150

Island Scribes
c/o 1000 E 98th Street, Brooklyn, NY 11236

The League of Handbinders
7513 Melrose Avenue, Los Angeles, CA 90046

Lettering Arts Association
303 Cumberland Avenue, Asheville, NC 28801

Lettering Arts Guild of Boston
86 Rockview Street, Jamaica Plain, MA 02130

New Orleans Calligraphers Association
6161 Marquette Place, New Orleans, LA 70118

Opulent Order of Practising Scribes
1310 West Seventh, Roswell, NM 88201

Philadelphia Calligraphers Society
P.B. Box 7174, Elkins Park, PA 19117

Phoenix Society for Calligraphy
1709 North 7th Street, Phoenix, AR 85006

San Antonio Calligraphers Guild
c/o 3118 Mindoro, San Antonio, TX 78217

St. Louis Calligraphy Guild
8541 Douglas Court, Brentwood, MO 63144

St. Petersburg Society of Scribes
c/o 2960 58th Avenue S, St. Petersburg,
FLA 33712

Society for Calligraphy & Handwriting
c/o The Factory of Visual Art,
4649 Sunnyside North, Seattle, WA 98103

Society for Calligraphy
P.O. Box 64174, Los Angeles, CA 90064

Society for Italic Handwriting, BC Branch
P.O. Box 48390, Bentall Centre,
Vancouver, B.C., Canada V7X 1A2

Society of Scribes
P.O. Box 933, New York City, NY 10022

Tidewater Calligraphy Guild
220 Cortland Lane, Virginia Beach, VA 23452

Valley Calligraphy Guild
3241 Kevington, Eugene, OR 97405

Washington Calligraphers Guild
Box 23818, Washington, DC 20024

Western American Branch of the S.I.H.
6800 S.E. 32nd Avenue, Portland, OR 97202

The Western Reserve Calligraphers
3279 Warrensville Center Road, Shaker Heights,
Ohio 44122

Wisconsin Calligraphers' Guild
2124 Kendall Avenue, Madison, WI 53705

**Calligraphy societies in Europe**

The Society of Scribes & Illuminators
c/o FBCS, 43 Earlham Street,
London WC2H 9LD

The Society for Italic Handwriting
69 Arlington Road, London NW1

The Mercator Society
Gaasterland Str 96, Haarlem, Holland

Bund Deutscher Buchkunstler
6050 Offenbach am Main, Hernstrasse 81,
W. Germany